D1126877

GPS: Global Positioning System

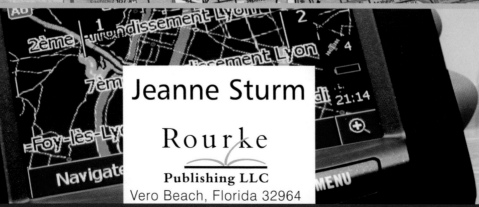

Jeanne Sturm

Rourke
Publishing LLC
Vero Beach, Florida 32964

www.rourkepublishing.com

PHOTO CREDITS: © Lorenzo Villavecchia: Title Page; © Galyna Andrushko: page 4; © Teze: page 5; © Hank Frentz: page 6; © Matt Cooper: page 7; © Valerie Loiseleux: page 11 bottom; © Avriette: page 11 top; © Photosky 4t com: page 12; © Mark Evans: page 13; © Konstantine Inozemtsev: page 14; © Andrey Volodin: page 16 top; © David Marchal: page 16 bottom; © Sergiy Zavgorodny: page 17, 25; © Scehardt: page 19 top; © The Aerospace Corporation: page 19 bottom; © Amy Walters: page 20; © Simone van den Berg: page 21 top; © Normon Pogson: page 21; © iofoto: page 23; © Stas Volik: page 26; © Gregory Johnston: page 27; © LWPhotography: page 28; © empipe: page 29; © Robert Dant: page 31; © ra-photos: page 32; © Rob Fox: page 33; © prism_68: page 34; © Lisa F. Young: page 35; © Ivonne Wierink: page 36; © Orange Line Media: page 37; © Ivan Cholakov: page 38; © Ariel Bravy: page 39; © Joroslaw Wojcik: page 42 top; © Krzysztof Krzyscin: page 42 bottom; © Martin Vegh: page 43; © Roberta Casaliggi: page 44; © Sean Locke: page 45

Editor: Nancy Harris

Cover Design by Nicky Stratford, bdpublishing.com

Interior Design by Renee Brady

Special thanks to the Aerospace Corporation

Library of Congress Cataloging-in-Publication Data

Sturm, Jeanne.
  GPS : Global Positioning System / Jeanne Sturm.
     p. cm. -- (Let's explore technology communications)
  Includes index.
  ISBN 978-1-60472-330-4
  1. Global Positioning System--Juvenile literature. I. Title.
  G109.5.S78 2009
  910.285--dc22
  629.46   2008012995

Printed in the USA

CG/CG

Rourke Publishing

www.rourkepublishing.com – rourke@rourkepublishing.com
Post Office Box 3328. Vero Beach. FL 32964

Contents

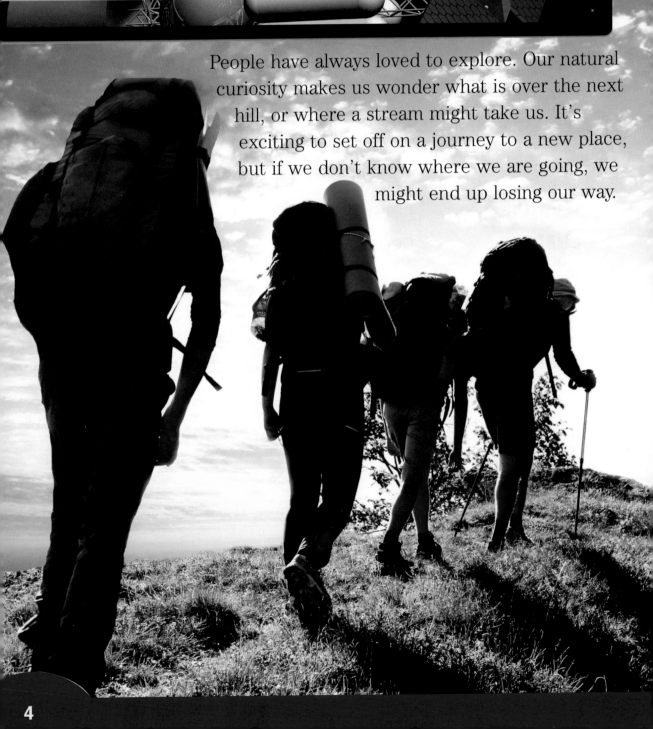

CHAPTER ONE

Finding Our Way

People have always loved to explore. Our natural curiosity makes us wonder what is over the next hill, or where a stream might take us. It's exciting to set off on a journey to a new place, but if we don't know where we are going, we might end up losing our way.

We can travel on foot, by boat, or by car. Sometimes, we choose to ride bicycles to reach our destination. We might even take an airplane or train to travel a long distance. Wherever we go, it's important to have a plan so that we don't get lost.

Early explorers used the Sun and the stars to find their way. Later, compasses were developed. A hiker could use a map to plan his route, and a compass to tell him in which direction he should travel. Maps and compasses are helpful, but a new technology can do much, much more.

The **Global Positioning System** (GPS) is a system of **satellites**, **monitoring stations**, and **receivers**. The United States government developed the technology for military use. In 1983, it became available to the public. Now, anyone with a GPS receiver can use the system for free.

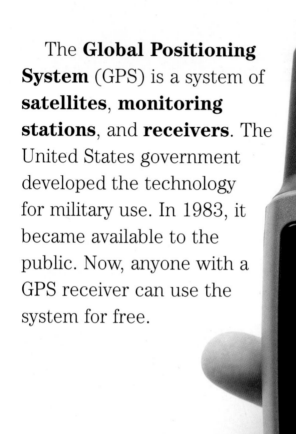

Many hikers carry handheld GPS receivers.

CHAPTER TWO

How GPS Works

Satellites

The Global Positioning System begins with 24 satellites. Each satellite makes two complete rotations around the Earth every day. Extra satellites have been put into orbit, so that they can take over when older satellites stop working.

The satellites are solar powered. Solar panels collect energy from the Sun, and use it to power the satellite. Each satellite carries four **atomic clocks** that send the exact time to GPS receivers on Earth. At the same time, the satellite is transmitting its location to the receivers. A GPS receiver will use this information to determine its own location on Earth.

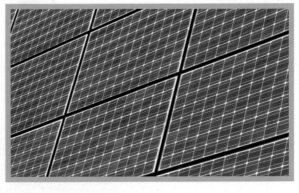

A GPS satellite is about 17 feet (5.2 meters) across with solar panels extended.

Fun Fact

Each satellite is fitted with small rocket boosters that are used to keep it flying accurately in its path.

Monitoring Stations

Monitoring stations keep the Global Positioning System running smoothly. Some are located in the United States, and others are situated elsewhere around the globe. Monitoring stations have been installed on Kwajalein, an island group in the Pacific Ocean; Diego Garcia, an atoll, or island, in the Indian Ocean; and Ascension Island, in the South Atlantic Ocean, among other locations. Tracking information sent from orbiting satellites to these worldwide sites is relayed to the Master Control Station in Colorado.

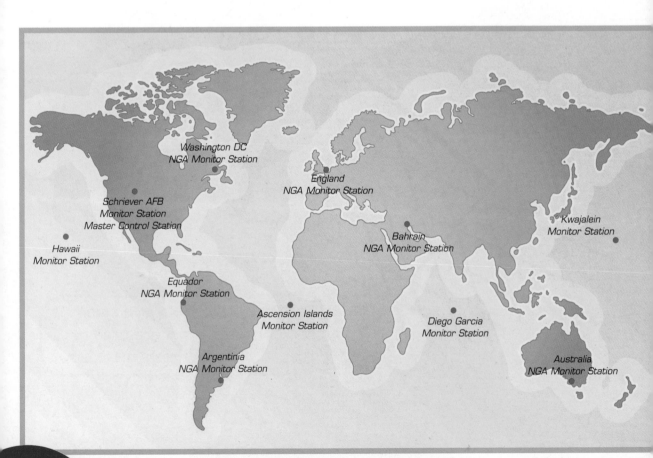

Washington DC
NGA Monitor Station

England
NGA Monitor Station

Schriever AFB
Monitor Station
Master Control Station

Kwajalein
Monitor Station

Bahrain
NGA Monitor Station

Hawaii
Monitor Station

Equador
NGA Monitor Station

Ascension Islands
Monitor Station

Diego Garcia
Monitor Station

Argentinia
NGA Monitor Station

Australia
NGA Monitor Station

The Master Control Station is operated by the 50th Space Wing, located at Schriever Air Force Base in Colorado. Men and women working at the Master Control Station send updated navigation information to GPS satellites. They synchronize the atomic clocks on board the satellites and monitor their positions in orbit. Without this fine-tuning, GPS receivers would lose accuracy over time.

The Master Control Station is located at Schriever Air Force Base in Colorado Springs, Colorado.

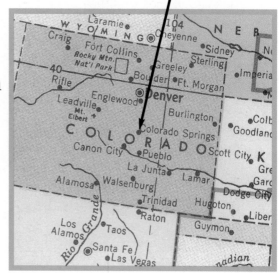

Receivers

The GPS receiver is the unit that you use. There are many types of receivers, but they all work in the same way. When you turn on your GPS receiver, the first thing it does is listen to radio signals to find out where the satellites are.

Satellites send signals that identify themselves and tell the exact time their signal was sent. Your receiver calculates how far away a satellite is by figuring out how long it took to receive the signal.

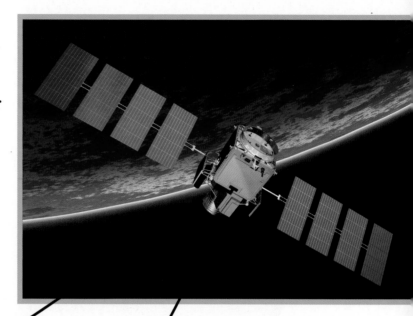

**satellite 1
11,000 miles
(18,000 km)
from satellite**

Information from just one satellite is not very helpful, though. Say the first satellite you detect is 11,000 miles (18,000 km) away. Your receiver can't tell you much except that you are somewhere in a big circle that is 11,000 miles away from the satellite.

A second satellite helps a little more. It might tell your receiver that you are 12,000 miles (19,000 km) away from it. This creates another very large circle. The area where you are standing is somewhere in the area where the two circles overlap.

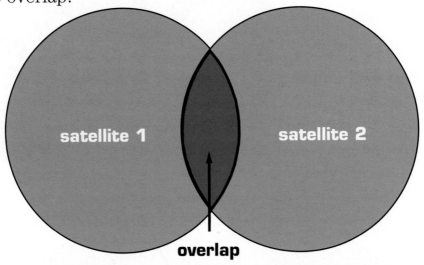

satellite 1   satellite 2

overlap

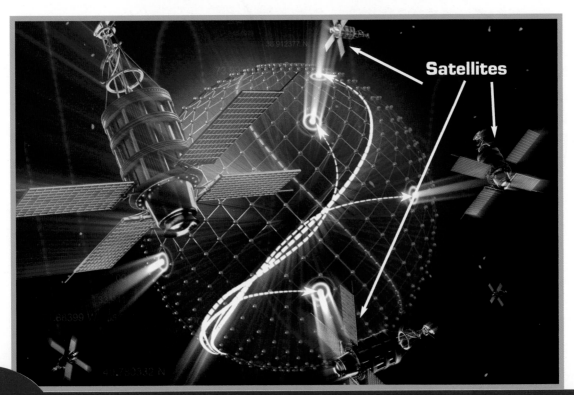

Satellites

It's the third satellite that finally pinpoints your location. Say the third satellite is 13,000 miles (21,000 km) away. The three circles all overlap in a very small area. This is your location!

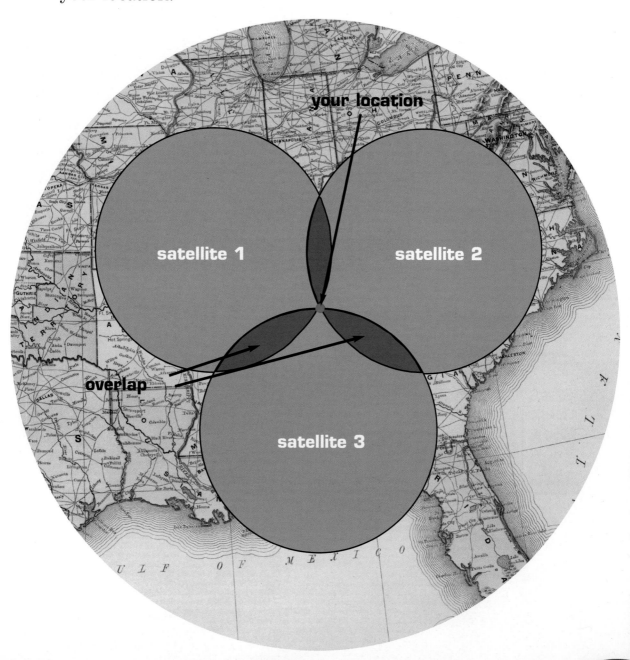

Three satellites send all the information your receiver needs to figure out your **latitude** and **longitude**. **Data** from a fourth satellite lets your receiver calculate elevation, as well.

Fun Fact

Your GPS receiver can tell you what time the Sun will rise and set wherever you are.

When you turn on the GPS receiver in your car, it needs to take a minute or two to locate satellites. Once it determines where it is, your receiver can pass along a lot of handy information. It will tell you your speed, in what direction you are traveling, and the distance to your destination. If you are at the beginning of a very long trip, you might be surprised when your GPS unit gives you an arrival time much earlier than you'd have thought possible. Remember, your receiver isn't thinking about the stops you'll have to make to fill up your gas tank and your hungry stomachs, or the traffic you might encounter along the way.

CHAPTER THREE

The History of the Global Positioning System

We live in a time when technology is rapidly changing. It wasn't so long ago that preparing for a trip meant making sure you had updated versions of the right maps. If you got lost, there was no such thing as a cell phone. You'd need to pull over and ask directions or find a pay phone and call for help. So how did the Global Positioning System come about?

In the 1960s, United States military branches worked on developing radio **navigation** systems. In 1973, the Air Force took all the information and put it together into a single program called the NAVSTAR (Navigation Signal Timing and Ranging) Global Positioning System.

The military was interested in using NAVSTAR GPS for navigation, but also for guiding weapons. Because the military didn't want an enemy to use GPS technology against us, non-military units were made less accurate.

Fun Fact

The first NAVSTAR satellite was launched in 1974, and the system was in operation by the mid 1980s. All 24 satellites were orbiting Earth by 1994.

Selective Availability

GPS technology was first developed for military use. Civilians could use the system, but the information they received was not as accurate as the military's. This was due to something called Selective Availability (SA). We could use our GPS units to find our location, but only within a little over 300 feet (about 100 meters) of our actual location. The information military users could get was much more accurate.

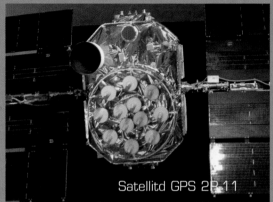

Satellitd GPS 2R-11

In May 2000, Selective Availability was turned off. Suddenly, even civilian users could enjoy accuracy within about 50 feet (15 meters).

"Lighthouses in the Sky
Serving All Mankind"

Dr. Ivan A. Getting
1912-2003

Dr. Ivan Getting, President and CEO of The Aerospace Corporation, came up with the idea of the Global Positioning System and worked for years to make his dream a reality.

Satellite GPS 2R-11 is fitted with an engraved plate honoring Dr. Getting, who died in 2003.

Reprinted with permission of The Aerospace Corporation

CHAPTER FOUR

Traveling by Automobile with GPS

Now that you understand how GPS works, it's time to explore the fun side of the technology. For many people, the receiver they use in their car is their introduction to using the system.

Have you ever driven to an unfamiliar place? Sometimes it can be confusing to navigate in a new city. If you have a GPS receiver, you can type in the address you're looking for and it will tell you how to get there, one step at a time.

What if you want to stop and buy flowers for Great-Aunt Lucy on the way to her house? Most receivers let you look for stores, restaurants, and attractions where you are, or where you will be later in your journey.

Is there only one brand of gas Dad will buy? Type in the name of the gas station, and your GPS will tell you where to find it.

All of the places you've located using your receiver are known as **waypoints**. Storing these locations on your receiver lets you save the information and return to the same spot at another time. Each time you enter a waypoint as a destination, the GPS will tell you how to get there from your current location.

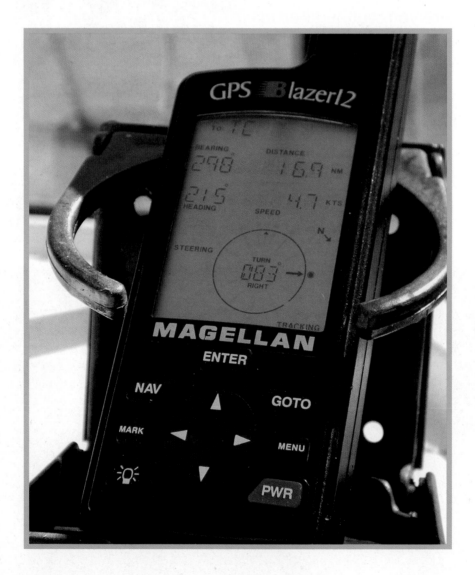

Your receiver can take you to the flower shop, locate a gas station, and find a favorite restaurant, all on the way to Great-Aunt Lucy's house in another city. It will even give you an estimate of what time you will arrive at her house.

CHAPTER FIVE

Enjoying the Outdoors with GPS

Hiking

Your GPS receiver can be especially useful on a hike in an unfamiliar area. Think about taking a walk in the woods. You follow a path into the woods and begin spotting trees, mosses, birds, and squirrels. After a while, you think you've spotted a rabbit behind a small bush, so you step off the trail to investigate.

You follow the rabbit as it hops away, leaving the trail behind, but after a few minutes you give up on finding that quick, little rabbit. You decide it would be smart to get back to the trail, so you turn around, only to realize you're not quite sure which way to go. Every tree looks unfamiliar, and the trail is nowhere to be found.

This situation could be a little frightening and dangerous. But, with a GPS receiver, you would be able to find your way back very quickly.

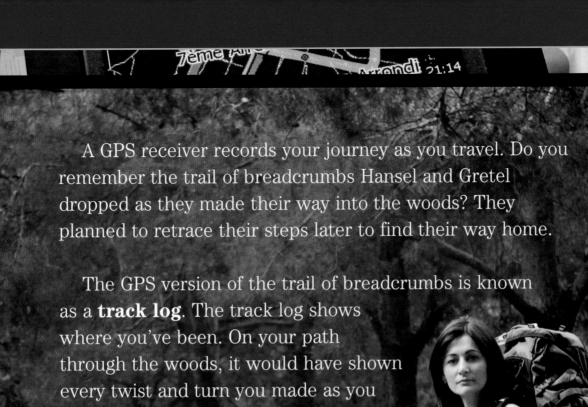

A GPS receiver records your journey as you travel. Do you remember the trail of breadcrumbs Hansel and Gretel dropped as they made their way into the woods? They planned to retrace their steps later to find their way home.

The GPS version of the trail of breadcrumbs is known as a **track log**. The track log shows where you've been. On your path through the woods, it would have shown every twist and turn you made as you followed that little rabbit around trees and over rocks. To find your way back to the path would be easy. Just retrace your steps along the ***breadcrumb trail***, or track log, shown on your GPS.

Boating

A track log can also be very helpful to boaters. Navigating a canoe or rowboat among small islands can leave a boater confused. Weather conditions such as dense fog or heavy rain might make it difficult to find the way back. But a boater who used his GPS would be able to find his way back to shore easily.

Fishing

Fishermen can use their GPS receivers to mark good fishing spots. Then, they can return to the same spot on subsequent trips, in the hopes of another good catch.

Navigating at Sea

Mariners and oceanographers use GPS data for underwater surveying and for marking hazardous locations. When a ship is at sea, knowing its speed, position, and heading helps sailors reach their destination safely.

Outdoor Sports

Athletes, such as golfers and bicyclists, benefit from the Global Positioning System.Golfers use GPS to measure precise distances from their ball to the hole.

Knowing how far his ball must travel helps the golfer select the best club.

Bicyclists rely on GPS data for up-to-date information that maps might not contain. Paper maps can become outdated, but GPS receivers can upload information from the Internet and keep cyclists on the right path.

Mountain bikers share favorite trails on Internet websites so others can enjoy visiting the same spots.

CHAPTER SIX

Geocaching

Have you ever gone on a scavenger hunt? You might have used a map as you searched for a list of treasures. If your scavenger hunt took place in the woods, your list probably included things like pinecones, acorns, or the feather from a bird.

A new sport uses GPS in a high tech approach to scavenger hunts. It is called **geocaching**. Geocaching gets its name from the prefix geo- and the word cache. Geo- refers to geography. A **cache** is a hiding place where hikers and campers place items for safekeeping. Sometimes campers place food in a cache to prepare for an upcoming camping trip. In geocaching, you would not place items in caches for your own use, but for others to find as part of the hunt.

Geocaching is a young sport. It started on May 3, 2000, when a man named Dave Ulmer hid a bucket of items in the woods outside Portland, Oregon. He posted its location on an Internet site. Within a day, someone found his cache of food, a compass, and a videotape. Within a few days, more caches had been hidden in other states. Within a month, someone in Australia had hidden a cache. Through the Internet, the popular new hobby was quickly spreading around the world.

Many people geocache in groups or with their families. It's a fun way to spend time together, enjoying the natural world. First, you'll need a GPS receiver. Try to choose one that stores waypoints as a track log, so you can retrace your steps after finding the

cache. Then, log on to an Internet site that lists caches in your area. You can choose an easy or difficult hunt depending on the abilities of your group.

Once you've decided on a cache, create a waypoint in your GPS unit by entering its latitude and longitude. Then choose a small item that you don't mind giving away. You'll be leaving this at the site for the next geocacher who comes along.

Using your GPS unit to guide you, begin your treasure hunt to the cache. You'll follow the arrow on your GPS as it brings you closer and closer to the point you entered earlier.

Finally, you'll find it! Open it up and see what wonderful trinkets others have left. Now comes the fun. You get to take an item with you from the cache. Just be sure to leave an item, too. One day, maybe soon, another adventurer will discover this cache, and they, too, will open it up to see what treasure awaits!

CHAPTER EIGHT
GPS at Work

GPS technology doesn't just enhance our enjoyment of outdoor sports. It also serves to makes our labor less difficult.

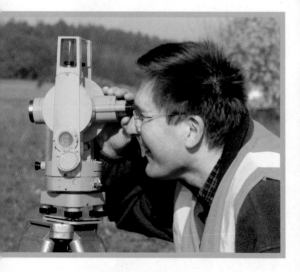

Construction companies use GPS to save time and plan accurately. Surveyors and mapmakers also benefit from the information.

Fun Fact

When the British and French decided to build a tunnel under the English Channel, they started digging from opposite ends. One crew began work in Dover, England, and the other in Calais, France. They used GPS receivers to check their positions as they worked. GPS data helped them keep their tunnels straight. The English Channel tunnel, or Chunnel, opened in 1994.

Delivery trucks and courier services find GPS data helpful in planning their routes. They can determine the safest and fastest way to get from one point to another, saving gas and time.

GPS technology helps us protect the environment. When a tanker spills oil at sea, buoys equipped with GPS receivers track the spread of the oil to guide cleanup operations.

Aircraft use GPS along with infrared scanners to locate *hot spots* and identify fire boundaries. Firefighters use this information to more safely and quickly fight the fire.

GPS-equipped balloons monitor holes in the ozone layer over the north and south poles. New satellites, launched in April 2006, use GPS to observe, research, and forecast hurricanes, typhoons, and other storms.

Aviators throughout the world use GPS. Use of the technology means there are fewer delays, because air space can be used more efficiently. This is especially helpful when winter storms affect flight schedules.

During Operation Desert Storm, U.S. military forces found GPS technology to be extremely valuable. Soldiers were able to maneuver in sandstorms and at night with the information the units provided. Ground troops carried GPS receivers, and helicopters, aircraft, and other vehicles were equipped with them.

Navy ships used the units for **minesweeping** and aircraft operations, and for meeting up with other ships at sea.

CHAPTER NINE

GPS Helps Save Lives

When disaster strikes, a quick response saves lives. Knowing the location of streets, buildings, and disaster-relief sites helps rescuers find survivors and get them the medical care they need.

Search and rescue teams used GPS to save lives after the 2004 tsunami in the Indian Ocean, the Pakistan-India earthquake in 2005, and the devastating hurricanes Katrina and Rita in the Gulf of Mexico region in 2005.

Scientists use GPS to study areas that are prone to earthquakes. GPS survey equipment helps measure the motion of faults in earthquakes. Scientists use what they learn to study how strain builds up slowly over time. They hope to be able to predict earthquakes earlier so that in the future more lives can be saved.

In a fire, every second counts. When someone needs an ambulance or a police officer, a long wait can mean trouble. GPS information helps police, fire, and emergency responders get there quickly in life or death situations.

CHAPTER TEN

GPS Units: Various Receivers for Various Needs

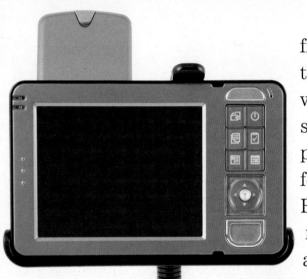

All GPS receivers use information from orbiting satellites to determine their location, but consumers will want to think about their own specific needs before making a purchase. Handheld units are ideal for hiking, cycling, and geocaching. Boaters will look for water-resistant marine units that map waterways and monitor depth. Automobile receivers come with preloaded maps. A voice will talk you through your route, turn-by-turn, as written directions are displayed on-screen.

Many of us were introduced to the Global Positioning System through handheld or automobile receivers. We find it interesting to know where we are and how long it will take us to reach our destination.

We can plan long trips based on the information we receive from GPS technology. We not only enjoy using the unit to locate favorite restaurants and stores, but also to explore and discover new areas and attractions.

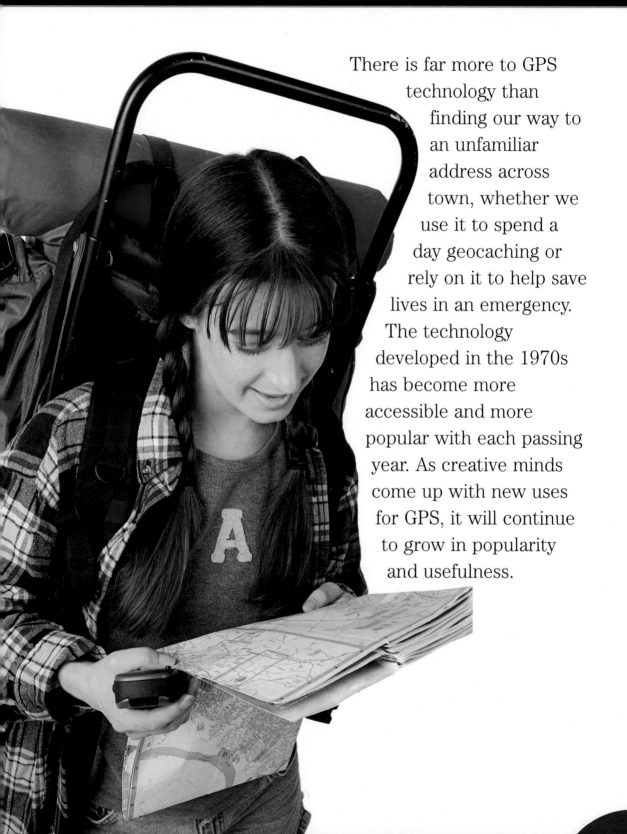

There is far more to GPS technology than finding our way to an unfamiliar address across town, whether we use it to spend a day geocaching or rely on it to help save lives in an emergency. The technology developed in the 1970s has become more accessible and more popular with each passing year. As creative minds come up with new uses for GPS, it will continue to grow in popularity and usefulness.

Glossary

atomic clocks (uh-TOM-ik KLOKS): clocks that have the ability to measure time very precisely

breadcrumb trail (BRED-kruhm TRAYL): the GPS display of the path a person has traveled

cache (KASH): a waterproof container that usually holds trinkets, a logbook, and a pencil for someone to find

data (DAY-tuh): information that is collected for a specific purpose

geocaching (JEE-oh-kash-ing): using a GPS receiver to locate a treasure hidden somewhere outdoors

Global Positioning System (GLOH-bul puh-ZISH-uhn-ing SISS-tuhm): a system where satellites orbiting Earth send information to receivers, telling them exactly where they are on Earth

latitude (LAT-uh-tood): a measure of a location in degrees north or south of the equator

longitude (LON-juh-tood): a measure of a location east or west of the prime meridian

minesweeping (MINE-sweep-ing): clearing mines (explosive devices) from sea lanes to protect ships as they travel

monitoring stations (MON-uh-tur-ing STAY-shuhnz): ground stations that track satellites and send information back to them to keep them running smoothly

navigation (nav-uh-GAY-shuhn): the process of planning a route with the aid of maps, compasses, or other devices

receivers (ri-SEE-vurz): the units, or devices, we use that take information from satellites to give us our position on Earth

satellites (SAT-uh-lites): objects that orbit the Earth

track log (TRAK LOG): the points stored on a GPS device that show the path a person has traveled

waypoints (WAY-points): specific points logged into a GPS receiver

Index

Further reading

Sherman, Erik. *Geocaching: Hide and Seek with Your GPS*. Apress, 2004.

Websites

www.wikihow.com/Go-Geocaching

www.howstuffworks.com/gps.htm

www.gps.gov

About the Author

Jeanne Sturm grew up exploring the woods, waterfalls, and riverbanks around her home in Chagrin Falls, Ohio. She earned her Education degree at Bowling Green State University and moved to Tampa, Florida, to teach. She began windsurfing, where she met her future husband. Now married, Jeanne, her husband, and their three children live in Land O' Lakes, Florida, with their dog, Astro.